A Day of It

A Day of It

poems

MICHAEL CHITWOOD

Louisiana State University Press
Baton Rouge

Published by Louisiana State University Press
lsupress.org

Copyright © 2026 by Michael Chitwood
All rights reserved. Except in the case of brief quotations used in articles or reviews, no part of this publication may be reproduced or transmitted in any format or by any means without written permission of Louisiana State University Press.

LSU Press Paperback Original

DESIGNER: Michelle A. Neustrom
TYPEFACE: Fournier MT Pro

Cover photograph by Wes Hicks on Unsplash.

Gratitude to the editors and readers of these journals, where these poems first appeared: *Appalachian Journal:* "A Bucket of Beans," "Maple Poindexter," and "Wayne Ray Nelson"; *Birmingham Poetry Review:* "The Barn," "Brightleaf," "Throwing the Snake," and "Whereabouts"; *Blackbird:* "First Loss," "The Potato Eaters," and "and Practicing His Signature"; *Chattahoochee Review:* "The Auction" and "Whom Some of You May Know"; *Poetry East:* "Amherst"; *Poetry Northwest:* "Frank Stanford and Gram Parsons Meet Little Walter"; *Prairie Schooner:* "Crafts" and "My Tree"; *Shenandoah:* "His Chair"; *Southern Poetry Review:* "Insomnia," "Men Next Door Talking While Working," and "The Shade of a Maple"; *Southern Quarterly:* "The Statue"; *Southern Review:* "The Old Singer"; *Tar River Poetry:* "Silent Letter"; *Texas Review Press:* "Virginia Opossum."

Thanks also to the staff at Louisiana State University Press for taking such good care of the poems in this book.

Cataloging-in-Publication Data are available from the Library of Congress.

ISBN 978-0-8071-8604-6 (pbk.: alk. paper) — ISBN 978-0-8071-8644-2 (pdf) — ISBN 978-0-8071-8643-5 (epub)

for Michael McFee,

brother in the art and keen-eyed first reader for, lo, these many years

CONTENTS

A Day of It

Whereabouts * 3
Barn * 6
My Tree * 7
Say of Me * 10
A Day of It * 12
The Old Singer * 13
The Potato Eaters * 14
Virginia Opossum * 16
A Bucket of Beans * 17

County Lines

June Fuller * 21
Sam Lavendar * 22
Martha Council * 23
Maple Poindexter * 24
Leah Sanders * 25
Raymond Muse * 26
Maynard Bedford * 27
B. Jackson Taylor * 28
A. Roland Davis, Esquire * 29
Wayne Ray Nelson * 30

The Right Knot

First Loss * 33
Whom Some of You May Know * 34
The Auction * 35
First Shift * 36
Silent Letter * 37
His Chair * 39
Anguish * 40

With

Whitetail * 43
When Turning Back Is Going On * 47
With * 48
Throwing the Snake * 49
Wings * 50

Can to Can't

Brightleaf * 55
The Statue * 59
Lightning * 61
When the Gods Came in Ships * 62

Cleave

Amherst * 65
Practicing His Signature * 66
Sketch * 67
The Joy of a Field of Corn * 68
Falling/Flying * 69
The Quick * 73
Insomnia * 76

A Sort of Census

Frank Stanford and Gram Parsons Meet Little Walter * 79
Crafts * 81
On the Porch with Franz Kafka and Little Walter * 82
On the Porch with Old Mr. Beesom * 83
On the Porch by Myself * 84

A Day of It

Whereabouts

Boy Scout campsite,
a grill/fireplace fashioned out of creek stone,
the creek just steps away
where the best spot was—
a shelf of flat stone that jutted into the stream.
You could crouch there,
wash your face with handfuls of cold water
and see yourself in that mirror.

*

Your eyes had to adjust,
coming in from the glare outside
to what he called "the shop."
It smelled of oil
and the woodstove he fired in winter
so his "projects" went year-round.
He knew the toolbox drawers like library shelves.
The workbench's wooden top was hammered matte,
the vise clamped on its corner ready to grip.
Time passed differently in that shed,
carefully, accurately, in no time at all.

*

There was never a finer throne,
the little collapsible stool
on that knoll
above the harvested cornfield,
waiting for doves, the 20 gauge across my lap.
September afternoon, warm,
the sunlight on the corn stubble a gold lamé,
the occasional report from another hunter's gun
on the other side of the field
and I could see up by the county road

the brick ranch house where the farmer's daughter
was going about her Saturday,
the young woman, now forty years my wife.

*

The tracks ran beside my freshman dorm,
though why we say "ran" I don't know
since there's nothing more still or steel
than railroad tracks.
Coal trains roared through the night
shaking our bunks, hauling us from sleep.
But warm afternoons, I'd take a break
from Chaucer or the Krebs cycle
and walk those creosote ties in their gravel bed.
It was goldenrod and milkweed on both sides.
It was climbing a horizontal ladder, the ties like rungs,
away from campus, that new life of learning, homesick.
There is no quiet like train tracks after the train has gone.

*

We made the hike up the hill
to all the old stones above campus
and by the gray obelisk
with the names of all the Confederate fallen
we clung to each other
not wanting the weekend over
and you leaving,
there among the dead never more alive.

*

I like it best in winter.
No boats zippering the lake with their wakes.
The bare trees give the deck
the full glare of the stark sun.
The summer birds have quieted.
Occasionally old man heron brings his arthritic flight
by the dock. He might stop
and go into his Zen pose,
that deep stare into the water.
Does he see himself
or what's underneath?

Barn

I rode you like a passenger ship
bound for new territory.
Your hayless lofts
were sun-slatted from the cracks
between the old boards.
I could almost feel the bulk of you moving,
setting out across time,
getting back to your busy days
full of calves and two mules
(I knew your story)
or maybe into your future: caved-in roof
and being burnt for volunteer firefighting practice.
I played the tines
of your rusty harp hay rake.
You were where I found
a clutch of kittens, soft nest of mewling.
A tomcat later found them:
I gasped at the slaughtered, bloody mess.
In one of your mangers
I hid my uncle's magazine
that like your loft window
gave me views of distant marvels.
You smelled like what I imagined
a grave would smell like,
old leather, burlap, ancient manure.
The grain of your boards was braille.
My fingers read the bloodline.
Except for me, no one used you anymore,
long quiet afternoons.
You were a kind of prayer.

My Tree

Mine by the claim of notice only.

*

Just off the left shoulder
of the Franklin Turnpike
if you're going north:
an oak,
midway between Danville and Callands.

*

To pay attention,
the wage of the world.

*

Perfect symmetry of its canopy
and solid girth of the trunk.
An artist's rendering of a tree
except it dropped its leaves in October.

*

I took the road for holidays,
Thanksgiving, Christmas, Easter,
"going home"
though home was not where I lived.

*

The lone tree
in the yard of a brick ranch-style.
It dwarfed the house.
I'm guessing they went to Danville for work.

*

I've never thought about what birds
have sung from its limbs.
I only *saw* it,
until now
when I'm not seeing it
except in the mind's eye.

*

A glimpse really:
rounding the bend at the farm implement store
going 55,
I would be past it in seconds.

*

Then, one trip,
I was coming back home,
the home where I lived,
so it was on the right;
it had been struck by lightning,
its perfect dome seared,
cracked apart and the trunk scorched.

*

Bypasser. Brief tourist
of the side of the road.

*

It remains
though I don't go that way as often.
Bedraggled, scarred, misshapen,
it lives.

Say of Me

She called the throat a "goozle pipe."

Of a certainty, she said,
"I know plime blank well."

"I thank you 'til you're better paid"
acknowledged a kindness.

She called gravy "sop"
and underwear "step-ins."
They went behind the sheets on the clothesline.

She looked under the bed
before getting in it.

The woman who had to pass her house to get to town
was a "roadrunner."

The Devil was "Old Scratch,"
which meant there *was* a Devil,
whom she feared more than God.

Thunder made her sit on the sofa.

She parboiled the squirrels her son killed
and made some sop.

She never drove, once she learned to drive
after her husband died,
over thirty miles an hour, mostly to church.
Slow gospel going and coming.

She sang "The Old Rugged Cross"
in a voice like a screen door opening.

She lived in one small place all her life.
She loved it and didn't want to leave
I know plime blank well.

A Day of It

He'd put on a pot of beans
and leave them to simmer
then rake a pile of leaves
from her old flowerbeds
and get a smolder started.
He'd cut a plug of Brown Mule
and tuck it in his cheek
then lean on the rake,
shifting the pile now and then
to let air to the fire,
arranging the sparks
and the afternoon,
letting the wispy drift of smoke
write a thin cursive note
across the yard.
Later, he'd go in to his beans
and a baseball game on the radio,
seeing the pitches and hits
on the diamond in his mind.

The Old Singer

Most of the time
it was like a desk
off to the side in the kitchen
where all things useful were done.
But sometimes she would clear it
of phone book and pencils and pocketknife
then bring the selected cloth
marked from the papery pattern
and arrange herself on the stool
as though she were part of the pattern
and begin to pump the treadle
that made the needle jump.
It was a marvel, that machine,
and how a dress or shirt came together,
the *tick, tick, tick* sound of it
more like time being made, not passing.

The Potato Eaters

We had a Ford Country Squire station wagon.
And a TV (black and white).
And good Sunday clothes.
But we still made a garden.
That's the way it was said,
"made a garden."
Green beans (rows and rows it seemed when weeding),
tomatoes, squash (everybody's squash came in—
that's the way it was said, "came in"—
at the same time so you couldn't *give* it away).
And potatoes.
My father and uncle shared a tractor
so in spring to lay off the furrows—
that's what was said, "lay off"—
one would go to the other
to see was he going to use the tractor a particular day.
Now here's the medieval part:
after Dad had plowed out the furrows,
he would take a bucket of 10-10-10
and hand cast it into the dirt,
his gloved hand rasping on the bucket bottom
to make sure to get it all.
Then it was my job to drag a big log chain
up and down the rows to mix in the fertilizer.
Where he came up with the chain idea I don't know.
Horse-like I pulled, both hands behind my back,
the chain trailing and chiming.
Then Dad went along with the seed potatoes
he'd sliced so that each piece had an eye.
That was the job I wanted,
cutting the eye pieces.
We gently covered them with the hoe.
When the potato bugs came for the plants,
I was told how to mix the Sevin Dust with water
and spray even up under the leaves. "Up under."

When the mixture got on my hands,
I'd eventually taste it at the back of my mouth.
Then in the fall he'd get the tractor again
and plow out the potatoes.
I came behind with my bucket.
At first it was hard to tell the spuds
from the clods of dirt,
but you got an eye for it after a while.
At the beginning of a row,
the potatoes gonged on the bucket bottom
but as the bucket got heavier it also got quieter.
I emptied the bucket into a basket at the end of the row.
Dad dug a pit and lined it with straw
and capped it with a piece of tin,
leaving one dark hole so that you could reach in.
Sent to get potatoes for supper
I knew each time my hand would not come back out right,
spider, wintering snake or just the dark would clutch it.
I guess with what we saved on food
we got an upgrade to a color TV.
Mom told folks she was going to let the radiation from the TV
cure the cancer the dye from all the Kool-Aid had given us
and so we gathered in Channel 7 News' backwash light
and ate thereof.

Virginia Opossum

hath an head like a swine,
tail like a rat,
of the bigness of a cat
   —John Smith

The dog charged
and it did what they do—
it died.
It's a trick maybe we should learn,
faint rather than fight.
It's served them well,
a fossil mammal, North American marsupial:
they survive, nocturnal,
and will eat anything, fruit or rotting meat.
But this one was ambling in daylight
which made me think something was wrong.
After I got the dog inside,
the scruffy little Jesus didn't resurrect.
Thirty minutes, it was still dead.
The dog was going nuts.
Finally, gloved, I lifted it by its thick bare tail,
a five-pound history lesson, colonists, Powhatan,
like us, grubber, mongrel,
and took it into the woods and tucked it in the fallen leaves.
Did it rise, return to its omnivore ways?
I don't know, but history says yes.
It was gone the next day.

A Bucket of Beans

Old newspapers cover their laps.
The women, it's almost always women,
bend to the bucket between them,
clutch a bristling handful of beans
and drop them on the sales and obits.
Their blind hands know the drill so well
there's no need for the women to look:
they string then pop the beans in thirds or fourths.
The hard shells ping the aluminum bowl.
They listen, advise, allow. The bucket empties.
The bowl fills. There, that's a half dozen meals.

County Lines

June Fuller

They were black, all black,
those old telephones,
black as Bibles.
And what was said
was gospel too, true or not.
You could ease up the handset
and hold down the button
then, real slow, let it up
and, party line, be in on the conversation.
Oh, you could get the dirt.
People would say what they thought
when they thought only one heard.
"Is someone on the line?" we'd say.
That's what we all wanted to know.
"Is someone listening?"

Sam Lavendar

We get together Wednesday nights
to make a little music,
middle of the week old-time string,
no electric.
Anybody can join in
so you never know,
but one week this old lady came to sing,
voice like the wind
coming round the corner of the house
on a night threatening meanness
and the songs from a place
you go only if you dare.
I tell you there's music
that can make you long for dawn.

Martha Council

I confess I like it best
here on Wednesday mornings
when I've come to clean up
the scraps left in the pews,
gum wrappers, mint cellophane,
and to polish the pulpit,
finger-smudged from the gospel's grab.
I shine it back to grain.
There's a hymn hum in the quiet
but it has to be
this still to be heard.

Maple Poindexter

This was before the sugar
took my one foot
when I worked the lunchroom.
There were some little ones
you just gave a little extra,
some that you knew
just another helping
might be the difference.
And it makes no never mind
if they even ate it all or not.
At least that's what I thought
I was doing with my days.

Leah Sanders

I don't know why Dad bought a guitar
with everything so spare.
I heard it cost five dollars
out of the Sears and Roebuck catalog.
It had no case
so it leaned in the corner,
all lacquer and hum.
It hurt my fingers, scored them.
But when he came in from work
on Friday of the first week
I had "Red River Valley."
He drank his coffee and nodded.
I guess he bought it
to tune his girl.

Raymond Muse

The dashboard is my office.
What can be measured
I have measured. Twice.
Cut once.
Plumb varies, site to site.
Better to be true
than to be right.
Every hammer has two ideas,
to pound in or pull out,
but the hammer don't decide.

Maynard Bedford

There's seven dogs in that pen
and I can tell you
in the blackest night
which one is baying
and the order the others will join in
and there ain't no choir
whatever stood in a choir loft
sung praises to the Lord
better than those seven together,
the scent hot in their strong finding it out.

B. Jackson Taylor

I like a neat workbench.
A man that don't respect his tools
don't respect what's done with them.
And I sweep up after
and leave the pile
if it's too small to warrant a proper throwing out.

A. Roland Davis, Esquire

At some point with the law
you must decide
whether to err on the side
that people are basically good
or basically bad,
for err you will
because of the circumstances.
There are always circumstances
and the light
on late fall afternoons
is blinding
in certain places along the road
where you might cross the line
into manslaughter.

Wayne Ray Nelson

At the lake,
after you've shot the bottle rockets,
the pop bottles' mouths
would be some hot kisses
and gone off is the crack and spangle
though you can still see it some
if you lay on the dock
and practice looking at where they sizzled to
and the lap of the little lake waves
is the gospel truth that you are being held up
by the old planking
and the rusty ripple-glubbing drums.

The Right Knot

First Loss

Only six,
what did I really know
about you?

Saws had taken fingertips.
That I knew
when you took my hand
to guide me across
the country store parking lot
to get a cold glass-bottled Brownie.

Stories came later,
not all angelic,
your and Dad's Christmas Eve hike
to get a jar of moonshine
and, almost back home,
the jar dropped and shattered.
The long walk back
to get another.

In the hall
outside my room,
Mom asked what I wanted to do.
I chose school
instead of the funeral.
The bus brought me home as usual.
The old car ghosted the driveway;
Grandma couldn't drive.
The rocking chair you made me
swayed through Saturday morning cartoons.

Sometimes I smell your cigarettes
and hear the pack crackle its cellophane.
Sometimes I hear you laugh
and start back for another jar.

Whom Some of You May Know

that he identified every unknown
tree as an ash.
He thought about such things
some some of you may know.
The seasons displayed in the branches.
Whom some of you may May.
A gentle man but with a fierce temper
when it came to lawn equipment
whom whom of you may know.
He would have heard the hum, um,
and the pause in all of that.
Some may know whom.
Some may know know.
The sum of you may ash
to display along a branch some May,
a quick green flicker of leaf.

The Auction

There comes a moment in the selling
of someone's life gatherings
when there's a box
of miscellaneous items
that was thought wouldn't move separately
and so were just jumbled together
and aren't even identified.
You just bid on the box,
the surprise and randomness therein.

And so it was I came to own a pine cone,
a small one she had thought to keep,
maybe picked up on a walk with her husband,
and a son or daughter boxed it,
because they knew its history
and couldn't throw it away.
A pine cone, this prickly bristle
I must hold so lightly.

First Shift

The smoke roiling from the huge chimney
is so thick and black it casts a shadow
which roils thick and black along the ground.
It's the medical center's smokestack
for the power plant.
The center requires its own power source
in case of an outage.
A spur of the railroad track
brings the train cars with the coal
that fires the plant.
The medical center's power plant is the terminal
for that spur.
Sometimes the coal comes topped with snow
from faraway weather.
It's early.
The doctors and nurses on the day shift
are walking in from the parking lots.
I don't know if they notice
the twin churning plumes.
Heart monitors chirp, early birds.
In one room, the room I'm looking from,
a TV has been on all night
bathing the man in the bed with light
as if it were the blue soapy water
from a nurse's aide's sponge.
The ancient fuel combusts
and darkens the air and the earth.

Silent Letter

Grant another day.
You think it works that way?
Here's a nice ptarmigan,

a feathered explosion
from the faithful underbrush.

*

His wrecking bar silent in the garage.
His wrenches agape.

*

He burned and shivered.
Nurses brought blankets
warm from the dryer.

Pneumonia.

*

The tools wait.
There's a knot
in the extension cord.

*

His hammer's handle
fits other hands

to knock together
or apart.

*

Now is never
enough

or is now
the right knot?

   *

Who ever has enough?
He was just here.
That's his wrench.

   *

Heart's gnome,
not every day
do we think of you.
But we think of you.

   *

Though through with thought
and out of hours,

he is not
out of ours.

   *

Hammer's knock.
Who's there?

His Chair

After lunch
and before he went

back to the fields,
he'd catch a nap

there, a quick fifteen
minutes he said

"percolated him." He's in
the fields for good now

and in that chair,
now in my living room,

his sleep keeps
its eyes on me.

Anguish

The word turns on the "g,"
turns like someone remembering
something forgotten, saying

"Oh," the backward glance
as though to look
would retrieve.

There's autumn in it,
the red, the umber,
the grief drifting.

It has a good mouthfeel
but the real of it
is in the limbs,

the weakness, ghost ache,
memory of having held
the weight no longer weight.

It begins in anger
but nods at the "g"
to longing, to wish.

There's a chair in a room,
a chair occupied
by its emptiness.

With

Whitetail

Does on wet asphalt, women in heels, stilty.

*

The explosion of mucus on the windshield
after the head slammed on the hood,
then the body under the compact car
and the car spinning on it.

While we waited for the police to arrive,
a guy skidded to a halt in a truck.
We thought he wanted to help.
He jumped out and ran over to us:
"Did you see?" he said.
"Was that deer shot?"

*

The night I'm sure our son was conceived
I heard them through the window screen
Cropping the short lawn grass. Whisperings.

*

The first I ever gutted. Surprised,
how hot it was inside.

*

When he came out at the end of his shift,
deputies waited by his car.
Someone had seen the rifle on the back seat.
"I wanted to get in a hunt before dusk," he said.
"It relaxes me to watch the fields."

*

In the tree stand, you hear before you see.

*

Each morning, checking the new shrubs,
the expensive leaves eaten down,
spreading the coyote urine pellets.

*

Interstate, a tractor trailer has left a long red smear.

*

The chained dog next door crazy with barking.
When I look out the window I see
a brazen doe facing off the dog,
striking at him with her hoof.

*

The blood-filled covering of the spring antlers. Velvet.

*

It was a long, heated discussion,
one woman in tears,
but the final neighborhood vote
was for bringing in bow hunters.

*

Downtown, rut full on,
a buck goes through the plate glass
of the hardware store.
"Probably saw himself," the game warden explained.

*

The print in mud, twin crescent moons.

*

Newlywed, hiking the far back fields
of the farm where we'd rented the tenant house,
I followed some track along a worn trail.
Finally looking up I saw the hunter in his stand.
He brought up the flesh pistol of his hand,
thumb hammer, index barrel,
and shot me. Then relaxed the gun and waved.

*

Almost tame, nibbling at the bird feeder,
a doe rises on her hind legs
as though ready for a dance.

*

In the small patch of woods
between this house and the next,
they seem to drift
this little bit of wild.

*

Startled by the door thud,
there's nothing more bolty.

*

Snow in the night, calligraphy, old writing all around next morning.

When Turning Back Is Going On

Across the path,
a spider has stretched
one web strand
and caught a single leaf,
a gate and padlock.

I ought to go on
I thought.
But don't,
the way so delicately shut.

With

I pull into the driveway
to find them standing in the yard,
a clutch like cousins at a family reunion,
a gathering of six does
with the startling albino in the middle.
The others are licking her,
a ritual bath
as though she's a princess
preparing to become queen.
Do they see her difference
or is it just her turn
for the comfort of the herd?
She doesn't preen,
just stands patient as a child
while the others give attention.
It's a painting come to life
a gift that, as if on signal, they all calmly turn
and walk out of the yard with.

Throwing the Snake

The man, his uncle,
jerked up the snake by its tail
and sent it sailing,

spinning rope-like,
a live whiplash
swishing through the air

and the boy, his nephew,
that the uncle had not seen
standing, frozen as the snake flew

toward him,
its spin singing
until it wrapped the boy's head,

a live cold-blooded blindfold
that immediately uncoiled
and fell to the ground.

What but primal impulse
makes a man throw a snake,
even a harmless black racer?

And what are the odds,
the truly odd odds
that a boy waits in its airborne path?

It is a kind of knowledge,
a base of the brain knowledge
that to be awake in the world

is to not be ready,
to be circumstantial,
to wear the living surprise.

Wings

BLUEBIRDS

I knew I would have to move the box
when I saw, for the second year,
the glistening length of him
pouring from the opening,
spiraling down the post
and starting his crawl across the yard,
inside him the downy chicks
making their one and only glide.

WOODPECKER

Two flaps and a tuck of wings
like a shuttle shooting through a loom
it knits the air.
I thought of her deft hands
and the seams coming together,
the sure needle's piercing work.

TURKEYS

Walkers mostly,
Stately, attentive,
members of a religious order
filing meditatively into a field.
But roused
they run for liftoff,
big wings thumping the air,
and sail only short distances
as though to fly
was a gift best used sparingly
and with a chortle of joy.

TURKEY VULTURES

Spooked from roadkill,
they struggle to climb,
lumbering as though not meant to fly.
But once aloft, they are effortless,
soaring gliders,
how flight is dreamed of
by the earthbound.

HUMMINGBIRD

First thing I can remember remembering.
It hung in her garden
at the trumpet blare blossom,
blur of wings but iridescent green body
and scarlet throat,
frantically still,
sipping a flower,
an ornament hung
on nothing's string.

Can to Can't

Brightleaf

"Smell that,"
the farmer I was working for said.
The ropey, toasted musk of curing tobacco wafted
from the tobacco barn.
"You know what that smell is?"
I shrugged.
"Money."

*

The first row I ever primed (I was fourteen),
riding that strange contraption, the primer,
its seat just inches above the ground,
working fast to get the bottom three leaves:
they ripened from the ground up
and the still-green top leaves were dew-covered.
It was like swimming,
my arms flailing and water pouring down
and when we got to the end of the row,
I was soaked,
my hands gummy with tobacco tar.
My head was spinning.
"It's the nicotine," Billy said.
"You just got your first buzz."

*

John Rolfe, the story goes, brought the seed
from the West Indies to Virginia.
It was the beginning of Empire,
the cash crop, gold leaf.
He later married Pocahontas
but she died in England,
slain by a European disease.
Later, back in Virginia,

Rolfe married his third wife.
The plants thrived.

*

It built cities—Richmond, Winston-Salem, Durham.
And homes, hospitals and universities.
It bought shirts, shoes and dresses,
food for the table,
and, early on, living human beings.

*

Thomas Jefferson noted
at the launch of the first James River bateau
that the big boat could haul twelve hogsheads of tobacco,
a thousand pounds each.
Three slaves—a steersman, a headsman and a third hand,
poled from Lynchburg to Richmond.
It was a two-week trip, down and back.
Out on the river, they had the tug of the current,
the gentle clap of the water against the boat,
the occasional rasp of rocks on the hull
and with no overseer were most free.

*

It was unusual
that none of the Thurmans smoked.
Months of seeding, planting, weeding, topping,
priming, tying, curing
and finally hauling to market their livelihood
to make the little white straws.
As we loaded the brightleaf for market,

out of nowhere, or maybe guilt, Billy said,
"You know what cigarettes are. Coffin nails."

*

Freed into servitude,
the sharecroppers had a saying:
they worked "can to can't,"
can see (barely) to can't see.
The children too.
After curing, Boss took the leaf to market
and returned with papers of the harvest's worth,
knowing none of them could read.
From their share, he took a portion for fertilizer
and the seed in the spring.
"Only fair," he said. "You've got a roof."
"Yes sir. But a low roof and nowhere else to go."

*

Danville Tobacco Market.
Here was where you made your year.
The farmers splayed the leaves on tarps,
a sampling of their crop.
The auctioneer's chant was a poem of money.

Cub reporter, I couldn't understand the song
but farmers and cigarette buyers
nodded or waved off the offers.
It was all subtle and wispy as smoke
and the bargain was for everything they had.

*

The Duke of Danville came home from the auction
drunk in his Sunday best
with a year's worth of meals in his pocket
and a new truck.
She was minding the pots and pans.
Huffing, she said,
"You know I worked as hard
as you did for that crop
and did the cooking too."
He bowed deeply,
flourishing his hat and said,
"And for that I thank you."

*

Driving NC 86 in the fall,
heading up to Virginia for Thanksgiving,
passing all the harvested fields.
The leafless stalks still stood,
sundialing their shadows on the ground,
counting hours, years, centuries
of this curious crop you could neither eat nor wear.
The stripped rows flashed by,
livings made and lives taken.

The Statue

It had a haversack and bedroll,
a musket and slouchy hat,
a bandolier of cartridges
and canteen stamped CSA—
in short, the entire equipage
a foot soldier needed
to stand his commemorating post
in front of the house
of traffic court, domestic disputes
and the occasional murder case.
It became part of the local weather,
less history than a porch pillar
until the unfortunate immigrant
rocky with street signs and traffic lights
let his half-pint pickup get loose
and rammed the plinth
to relieve the private of duty,
his hatted head rolling to the courthouse steps.
Then what had been mostly ignored
became of great concern:
Should it be restored,
this stone cipher of a war
that wasn't, well, waged for the best reasons?
Was this an attack,
this foreign national
armed with our own Chevrolet?
Everyone had their say.
Forgotten pride and lost causes
and art, let's not ignore art,
stirred the blood
and moved the citizenry
such that a collection could begin

and noble stone again be found
and the silent past
again cast its shadow,
a sundial for the day's hours.

Lightning

This must have been how it happened,
back in the used-to-be,
when gods regularly appeared to us
to either forsooth or forsake us.
I took the shortcut through the woods
and halfway, the apparition.
From the corner of my eye
I took it for a person, naked.
Then I saw it was a tree,
but lightning-blasted,
all its bark blown off.
The "skin" underneath was so pale and smooth
it looked alive, which it no longer was.
Not the tallest tree in the woods
nor with the biggest girth
but somehow chosen from all the others
to appear to me, for a second,
the goddess's lovely supple arms
and lithe trunk glowing
so that I could, almost, believe.

When the Gods Came in Ships

They had no names
for the devils of this hell,
salt-sprayed, chafe of sandy scrape,
the snarls of grabbing vine,
saw-edged fronds of grasses and palms
and prickly pine boughs swatting their faces.
Through this sharp scrub
they could hardly pass
and almost invisible swarms
stung and bit,
fed on sticky skin, drew blood.
They yelped when a serpent slid
through whispering grasses and puddles
or worse, cocked for a strike.
What could be worse than this?
The land lashed them
and made them so angry,
they decided to seize it.

Cleave

Amherst

Thinking in an imagined cottage,
when is enough enough?

I am my own Emily—
spinster to the spidered infinite.

The winter light is lavish,
blue shadows on snow,

the silver branches like sketches,
the eyes always with their handiwork.

When is enough enough?
Lace, frill, scrim of the dust of snow.

A village is too much.
Even to hum is lush.

Cupboard, shelf paper, teacup.
When is enough enough?

Practicing His Signature

Each time, before he put nib to paper,
he'd swirl the pen without touching down,
like a batter taking practice swings,
then he'd commit the ornate T,
all curve and slant,
and then the W, a march of waves,
each initial properly dotted with a period.
Then the surname, half Palmer, half Hancock,
loop-de-loops and forward rolls.

I saw him do it any number of times.
Take out a yellow legal pad
and lift up the first blank page,
he never wrote on that,
then sign his way into two columns of himself,
studying each line after he finished it
and then move on
until he had a page of the shortest life sentences.

Why that empty guardian sheet?
To hide the vanity? Or just protect his good name?
He took pride in his flourish
but no one else needed to know.

Sketch

Somebody waters the plant,
or oils it, maybe.
  —"Filling Station," Elizabeth Bishop

Ms. Bishop, this morning I'm thinking of my mother-in-law.
A farmer's wife, she used to sketch the calves
so they could be registered.
Holsteins, they had to have black and white
in the right places.
One black foot I think. Black patch on one shoulder.
And she gave them names, family names, for registration too.
I imagine it was quiet in the calf barn,
maybe the rattle of a suckle bucket now and then.
You could have felt all the lives that came before you
and all that would come after in that quiet,
in the milk sop and sawdust of those stalls.

You would have liked her, Ms. Bishop.
She, like you, noticed what most people
allowed themselves not to see.
Her husband used to say she took on "cases"—
women whose lives needed sketching too,
needed to be filled in a little.
I'm thinking she sang to the calves,
those future mothers, milk-makers.
They would grow into 1,500-pound slow amblers,
walking into the milking parlor,
hocks splattered with mud and manure.
Not awful at all, dirt-rich and pungent,
cheerful in a daily way.

The Joy of a Field of Corn

You can tell,
this farmer admires straight rows.
Topping the hill
and looking down on the field,
take in
the chest-high stalks marching
in tight, sharp ranks,
already tasseling out,
the blades of the fodder deep green.
Old McDonald knows
that you can, if you take the bother,
see his attention to the task.
I see his silent delight
in having done a thing right.

Falling/Flying

> *Sparrows were feeding in a freezing drizzle . . .*
> —Howard Nemerov

This dark spot
on my shirt

only moments ago
was snow

that moved slantwise
and like a moth

soft landed.

*

"Why is it we always want the clouds to look like something? Famous people. An animal. Why can't clouds just look like clouds?"

We were leaning on our shovels. Leaning on shovels always leads to philosophical discussions. Well, technically they weren't *our* shovels. They belonged to the highway department, in the same way, I suppose, that I belonged to the highway department that summer, at least for eight hours every day, every weekday, which is how someone you never otherwise would have met comes into your life and asks a question that you will carry like a folded letter in your wallet for as long as you live, and the clouds billow and drift, vaporizing in their magnificence.

*

Silk

is what it's called
because it looks it

and lifts
from the split pod

to drift
in its aliveness,

a feathery
almost creature.

floating
with its seed.

It goes
to thrive.

                    *

In my dreaming,
the rain on the deck
I could hear through the screen door

became applause,
a standing ovation,
the rain so upright.

                    *

It was called the Soldiers' Home. The war had just ended and the wounded came there. Young and unmarried, she needed work. She never said much about the year she was there or what exactly she did.

A year after she returned, and six months a newlywed, a man from the train station called and said a crate had arrived for her and she needed to send a truck for it.

It was a pipe organ, from one of the soldiers. There was no letter, just his name on the bill of freight. She explained nothing, but put the instrument in the living room. Later, her daughter learned to play.

Sometimes, hanging out clothes, the sheets flapping like sails, she would turn when from the house she heard the deep oboe moans.

*

"Shattercane," he whispered,
staring out the window at the cornfield.
It was as if to say the name too loudly
would shake that cunning stalk
and cast its seed among the rows.
"Shattercane." It came for him
with its determined life.

*

We were laying sewer line and in places the ditch had to be five, six feet deep to get the grade right. There had been little rain and the earth was powdery. The foreman said we were always to use the trench box, but it was a pain, getting it chained up to the backhoe boom and then guiding it into place to lay two or three joints of pipe. And the foreman was a priss, college grad, safety regs this, safety regs that. He was off with the big boss looking at some new equipment. We figured to hell with the box.

Clements said no sweat and was down in the ditch guiding the male end of the pipe into the female. He was a quick monkey. Nobody quicker.

One side of the ditch gave way and Clements was buried before anyone could even yell look out. We dug with shovels but mostly our hands, everyone on their knees, both arms going, some were asking the Virgin for help, others just Goddamning, Goddamning to Hell.

When we got to him, he was on all fours, hunched over the pipe. He'd used his body to make just enough space to breathe and we pulled him out and Jesus if it wasn't like a man coming up out of his grave.

*

At the stoplight, I see
a swarm some bush has let go.

It's crossing the road,
indifferent to traffic,

so light and numerous
it swirls

around the ponderous cars.

The Quick

WAYWARD

Having left the road
I wade in the weeds,
July tall, itchy.
I wonder if a tick
waits on one's tip.
It's the little things
that can smell blood.
I didn't know where
the road was going so
might as well wander
to the not here, to the
not there, to where it was
I didn't know to go.

*

THE SHADE OF A MAPLE

It's always Sunday afternoon here,
family reunion lawn chairs gathered.
You're in this photograph
because of the ordinariness of who you are.
For now, you're all here,
all being those who call themselves all.
It's cool in the shade.
In an hour or so, you'll leave.

*

MEN NEXT DOOR TALKING WHILE WORKING

I don't know what they're building or adding on to.
The bits I hear are the everyday nothingness.
One says something about measuring,

the other something about cutting.
They're quiet when using the hammers,
except for the hammers.
I imagine nails spiking their mouths,
the efficient use of the body.
It might rain.
They could maybe finish tomorrow if it does.

*

THE ROAD

What is taking so long,
stalled here, the road
brought down to one lane?
I want to be on my way.
For these men, this is their day,
summer heat above, hot asphalt below,
rolling out repair, making smooth,
making straight, the slow no-go
of new road. The flagman
shows either "Stop" or "Slow."
Why is being still so lasting?
We are fast in our pause,
in a line that is going
in its going nowhere.

*

TOMATO ON THE WINDOWSILL

Juicy Buddha,
if you look long enough
you can see it ripen:

vine-plucked,
it *oms*,

this globe, this planet
in orbit so slow
it seems still

as out the window
the summer backyard flashes by.

*

QUEEN ANNE'S LACE

To be so quiet,
like the doilies
my grandmother crocheted,
letting the needles click-tick
time away on something
to gussy up end tables,
completely useless,
like these weeds
cars zoom by,
the delicate blooms,
white, lacy, brief,
this morning
I've stopped to notice.

Insomnia

The night has but one hour,
but it is a long hour,

afloat in the little boat
that drifts of its own accord

as the stars scroll by,
visual braille.

There's a tune, no words,
that walks on the water.

You can't quite make it out,
something in the low register.

It's as if moss were humming
or the willow whips are strummed.

The boat turns,
first clockwise then counter.

What you have to answer for
or answer to is on the dark shore,

not far, but out of sight.

A Sort of Census

Frank Stanford and Gram Parsons Meet Little Walter

It was winderous, even the bare branches a-shaking.

The Indian took out a chicken foot and scratched his neck with it.

There was some men working on a bridge and below one man's job was to wait with a boat in case someone fell.

Spike said things go slant sometimes.

Man hands you a pocketknife with the blade closed you hand it back with the blade closed. Open, open.

The Mississippi saxophone runs on breath coming and going.

What light does on water is a manifestation.

Men working, they talk about dogs; they talk about their mamas.

A little boat is jostlesome.

Water under the bridge, my friend, that's what a bridge is for.

The Indian said the old ways were overrated, nobody ever mentioned all the coughing.

Five dollars says I could survive a fall, rocks and all.

Who decides where a bridge needs to be?

The man with the boat's job was to be on the job.

From the bridge the water looks spanglety.

One guy had a cross tattooed on his back. He just had to know it's there.

Men working on a bridge don't cross it.

When you go, what you leave goes with you.

Crafts

First Saturday in April now
the churches have a bazaar
in Weave Room 1,
the looms long gone,
the cavernous room
with the varnished floor echoey
until the craft booths are set up.
At least the building gets some use.

Some use, he thinks, is what we were
in the days when the building roared
with the thrashing of the looms.
The jobs have gone elsewhere
was what we were told,
as if what our lives had been
were children grown up
and moved away,
married to strangers.

On the Porch with Franz Kafka and Little Walter

All day it's been trying to rain,
the sky the back of a mirror, unreflective.
A crow is run-hopping across the lawn, chicken-like.
Why doesn't it just fly?
The dog is thunder-shy, spook saddled;
he porch haunts.
If I heard what he hears
I'd come up with a better answer
for what's going to happen and when.
I don't and won't.
Still there's something grumbly in the cloud bulk,
something thinking of tearing a limb from the poplar.
The leaves worry, shaky hands.
If the trees had pockets, they'd go for them.
The dog is cock-eared.
All day, the sky is rain-tinted, but no rain.

On the Porch with Old Mr. Beesom

And I was with my grandfather
as it was his custom in those days
to take me with him on his rounds
though it seemed to me we just wound up places,
a store with a soda cooler
or someone's house as was the case this time.
It was a sort of census I suppose
and Mr. Beesom was saying, "You see
that dog there," pointing to a black short-hair
that was asleep on the porch in a patch of sun.
"There ain't no telling what's put in it breedwise."
He also said something about the Raleigh man
with his salve and pills coming by and how the dog
was all wag when he did and what's to be made of that?
Finally I asked Granddad if Mr. Beesom
was talking or singing as he stayed in time
with the rocker's creaking runners
and Granddad lit another Lucky and let it
have its say until time enough had passed for my question to waft away
and then we had to be going it seemed
because all that needed accounting for had been accounted
and we were done doing whatever we were doing
on that Lucky Strike afternoon ramble.

On the Porch by Myself

In the house just now
back through the screen door
is that someone moving around?
No, just the tumble of ice
from the ice-maker.
Across the cove, two men are talking.
Their voices walk easily across the water.
They are discussing a pulley.
Its cables screech in lifting a boat.
Friday morning, people are out and about.
The dog is pacing, ready for a walk.
I'll keep my spot just now,
a notch in the going-onness.
"Scotch that tire," my father used to say
to keep a wagon from rolling,
a temporary stop, leaned against.

www.ingramcontent.com/pod-product-compliance
Lightning Source LLC
Chambersburg PA
CBHW030122170426
43198CB00009B/706